AF573802

the narrow streets

by
KENNETH McNALLY

blackstaff press belfast 1972

Published by Blackstaff Press Limited 84 Wandsworth Road Belfast BT4 3LW

SBN 85640 002 5

Set in 11pt Press Roman by Blackstaff Press and printed in Northern Ireland by Belfast Litho Printers Limited.

THE NARROW STREETS is an account in words and pictures of a part of Belfast which has survived, by accident rather than by design, the urge to rebuild and do away with the old, unfashionable, and on the face of it unfunctional aspects of the city. It is a story of the High Street entries, in particular those connecting High Street with Ann Street, though other peripheral passageways radiating out from here also come under discussion, all being in some way linked with the social and economic growth of Belfast from the seventeenth century to modern times.

The object of this account is to place the High Street entries in their geographical and historical perspective, while note is taken of their changing names in so far as this relates to life in the developing town. Where the field of folk lore is concerned, much has already been documented on the subject by local writers. One has only to mention such names as John J Marshall, Richard Hayward, Cathal O'Bryne and Colin Johnston Robb to recall the source of many informative and highly evocative tales associated with these little streets and the characters they nourished. A list of articles of related interest is contained in the bibliography at the end of this book.

THE EARLY TOWN

The early town as it took shape in the seventeenth century was, as it continued to be for some 200 years of its development, enclosed by the boundary thrust up by a prehistoric coastline, and rested on the soft yielding slob lands that were to prove problematic for modern town builders. When Arthur Chichester set about establishing a permanent settlement here shortly after 1603 - ten years before Belfast received its charter - the site consisted of little other than a handful of poorly constructed cabins huddled along the Farset River near the point where it entered the Lough. Apart from a picturesque setting there was nothing to indicate the viability of the undertaking or give one to suppose here was the essence of a future city of consequence.

From the outset growth appears to have been steady, and building, as far as can be determined from the few contemporary accounts in existence, followed a prescribed and orderly plan, though in retrospect it might be seen to lack the element of architectural control that appeared in later centuries. Thomas Phillips' map of Belfast in 1685 shows an uncluttered prospect in High Street and the surrounding area. Buildings of sturdy and even imposing construction are indicated, even at this early date, and there is an air of spaciousness that was to disappear in later years as the township expanded and began to utilise all available building ground. Our narrow streets did not then exist, though they might be said to have had their embryonic beginnings about this time, since many of the houses fronting onto High Street had little gardens through which public rights of way were gradually established. In time these rough paths became the well-trodden thoroughfares known as the High Street entries.

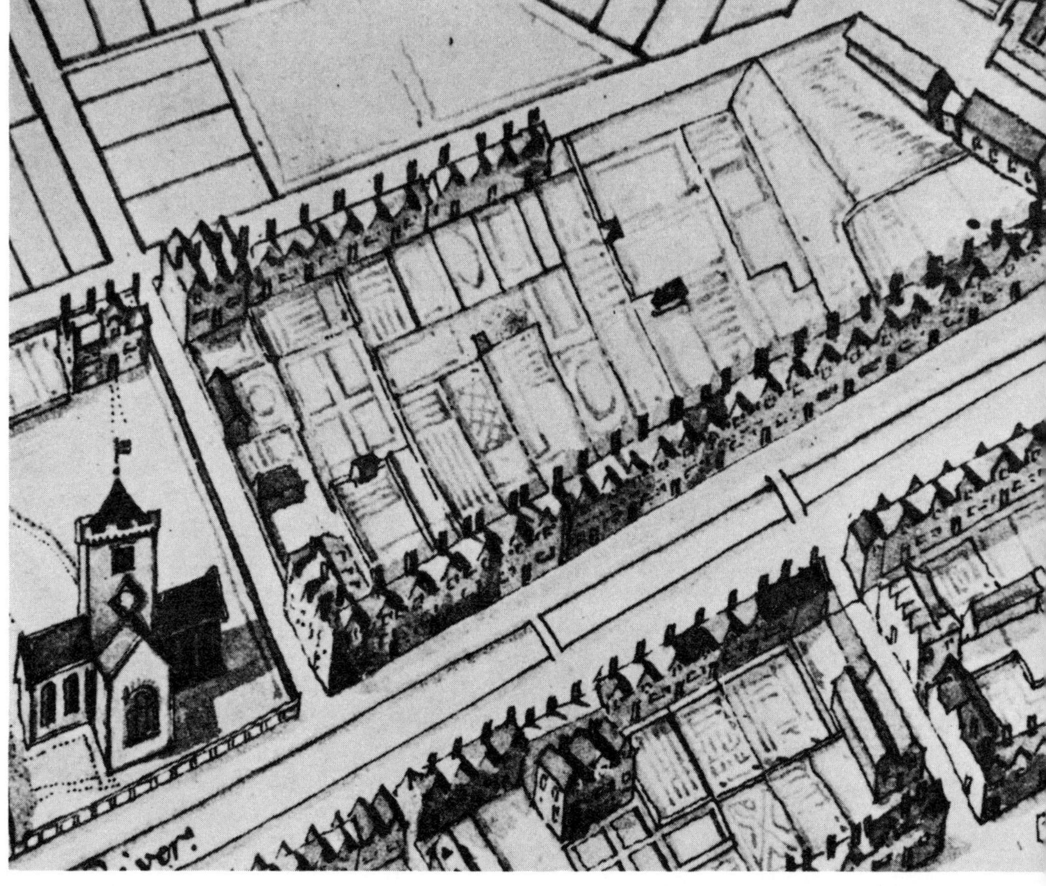

hillips' map of 1685: the private ardens belonging to houses in High treet and Ann Street are clearly efined. Features suggestive of aths are indicated, and some of the ardens appear to enjoy the privacy f a walled enclosure. The tall building at the top right of the picture is e old Market House.

By the early 1700s, trade in Belfast was increasing, though it had not yet reached the flourishing state it was to know in the latter half of the century when a number of factors, not least the arrival of cotton spinning, contributed to an economic stability that was to be reflected in material improvement within the town. But even during the first quarter of the eighteenth century the effects of commercial growth were apparent in the pattern of public and private building. Where, thirty years earlier, there had been conspicuous open spaces between the houses forming the nucleus of the trading centre. John MacLanachan's map of 1715 indicates that these were now being absorbed into the spread of urban development.

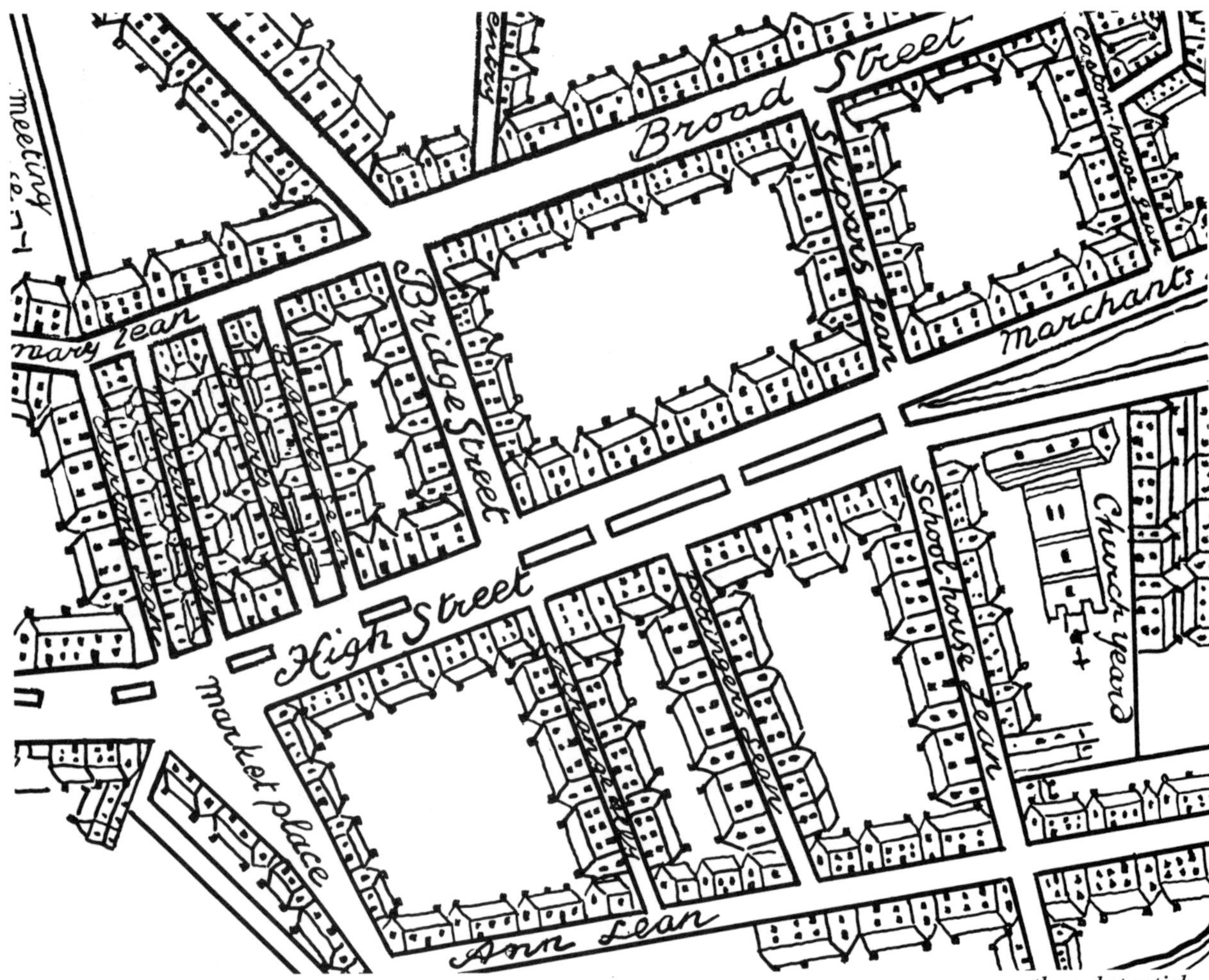

MacLanachan's map of 1715: the substantial increase in building in the thirty years that have elapsed since Phillips' map was drawn is apparent. Entries (shown as lanes and alleys) are beginning to take shape along the north and south sides of High Street as open ground is developed.

If MacLanachan's map is to be interpreted literally, most of the buildings in High Street were of two stories, and two of three stories are also shown. Ann Street, as might be expected from its subordinate role to High Street, consists of many single storey cabins and some two storey houses. It was at that time called Ann Lane, and along its south side buildings (absent from Phillips' map of 1685) are just beginning to fill up this sector prior to the formation of Telfair's Entry and Cooney's Court. Houses and stores already enclose the area bounded by High Street, School House Lane (Church Lane), Ann Lane and Market Place (Cornmarket). Two substantial passageways - Exchange Alley and Pottinger's Lane - bisect the phalanx of buildings on either side of this square and can be regarded as the first of the entries to assume permanent form in the centre of the town. Along the northern edge of High Street were a number of small passages and alleys leading to Rosemary Lane and Broad Street.

High Street, with its prominent Market House, was the hub of commercial life in Belfast in the eighteenth century. Merchants and shopkeepers congregated in busy groups along its length, particularly at the Stone Bridge (situated at the junction of High Street and the present Bridge Street), and in the open air bought, sold and bargained their way to financial success or obscurity. In 1770, the Sovereign of Belfast, who was also Clerk of the Market, emphasised the relative importance of the area when he ordered the sale of

> 'Fresh butter, cheese, fish, pigs, geese, turkeys, hens, eggs, chickens, wild fowl, conies and other dead victuals in no other place but High Street, and on the bridges built over the river from Pottinger's Entry[1] to the west end of the Stone Bridge, where the yarn measurers, town sergeants, and overseers of the market will be, to weigh butter, count suspected yarn, oversee and prevent disorders and disputes.'

High Street in 1786: buildings of three and even four stories are shown; the Farset River has been enclosed along much of its length, and an abundance of traders' sign-boards are in evidence.

Through time, as needs and fashion demanded, trading spilled over into the convenience and shelter of the several passageways and courts linking High Street with Ann Street, once private accesses to houses, but now integrated into the hustle and bustle of everyday affairs. Perhaps significantly, Ann Street was known as 'the back of the green' in the eighteenth century, even though the 'green' to which it referred was already disappearing under the foundations of new buildings. Ann Street was also called Back Street (an allusion to its subordination to the more important High Street, which in consequence was called Front Street), and, later, Bridge Street, since it led directly to the old Long Bridge at one time.

Houses opening onto High Street and Ann Street had restricted frontages, so that as these important thoroughfares filled up with buildings the only opportunity for enlargement lay to the rear. Often extensions were continued backwards for some considerable distance, especially so in the case of business premises comprising workshops and stores. As time went by adjoining tenements and their offshoots were

drawn together into a complicated network of interconnecting offices, open yards and dwellinghouses. The sole approach to these was through the entries formed by the juxtaposition of one building alongside another and from the deviation apparent in these passageways it is clear that they were the consequences of, rather than the reason for, the conglomerate development within.

High Street in the 1970s: only in recent years have modern buildings radically altered the skyline familiar to nineteenth century townsfolk.

Pottinger's Court, off Pottinger's Entry, 1971.

Wilson's Court, as it may have appeared at the end of the eighteenth century.

TRADE AND SOCIAL CONDITIONS

The entries, as they were now termed locally, soon gained credence as right and proper places of business and can therefore be regarded as strategic centres of trade in the expanding town. They were also becoming residential areas. Wealthy merchants anxious to be in close touch with the commercial life of Belfast found it expedient to live in proximity to their business premises. By so doing they not only maintained contact with day to day development affecting their own individual enterprises, but also contributed to the foundation and growth of a strong body of influential citizens capable of lending weight to the many municipal issues of the day. It was inevitably from their experienced ranks that many of the town's future leaders, administrators and visionaries were drawn: visionaries, to give but one example, like the inspired group of men who launched the noble enterprise that became the Belfast Charitable Society for the care of the poor and needy in the second half of the eighteenth century, and in so doing revealed a rare sense of public duty and social concern for what must have seemed an insuperable problem at the time.

The High Street entries seen from above: a mixture of twentieth, nineteenth, and even eighteenth century building.

Pottinger's Entry, about 1800.

Gradually the entries filled up with a casual alignment of offices, stores, taverns and houses as commerce took on a more intense expression of urgency. In the eighteenth century Belfast was intent on forging crucial links with America and the West Indies and by the end of the century at least thirty ships from the port were engaged in trade on these routes. Communication with Britain was also vitally important. Belfast relied heavily on its imports which, as reported by Arthur Young in 1776, consisted of 'rum, brandy, geneva and wines ... coals from Britain ... iron, timber, hemp and ashes from the Baltic ... barilla from Spain ... tea, raw sugars, hops and porter, the principal articles from Great Britain ... from North America, wheat, staves, flour and flax seed'. Export wealth was measured mainly in linen, but other commodities, notably agricultural produce, were also significant contributors to the export economy. Sugar refining, too, was expanding in the town; the industry had been pioneered by George Macartney in the latter half of the seventeenth century with the building of a large sugarhouse which was to give the name to one of the best known of the entries.

The eighteenth century was the age of the trader's signboard. Shop windows were small and gloomy and offered little opportunity to display goods to their best advantage, so that the sign suspended over the doorway became an important means of attracting customers inside. It is well known that the *Belfast News Letter* was printed at 'the sign of the peacock' in High Street; indeed that newspaper still proudly carries the emblem on its front page. Its advertising columns of two centuries ago indicate an age of eloquence absent from much of to-day's salesmanship. Consider, for example, how a rather mundane merchandise like ironmongery was elevated by an evocative business address in 1772: 'Thomas Lyle', it read, 'at the Golden Saw, next shop to the Orange Tree'. A decorative woodcut - a facsimile of the actual signboard - accompanied the advertising copy (it was one of the few newspaper illustrations to appear at that time) and doubtless worked wonders for the future success of Mr Lyle's business. It may be recalled

Trader's sign, 1772.

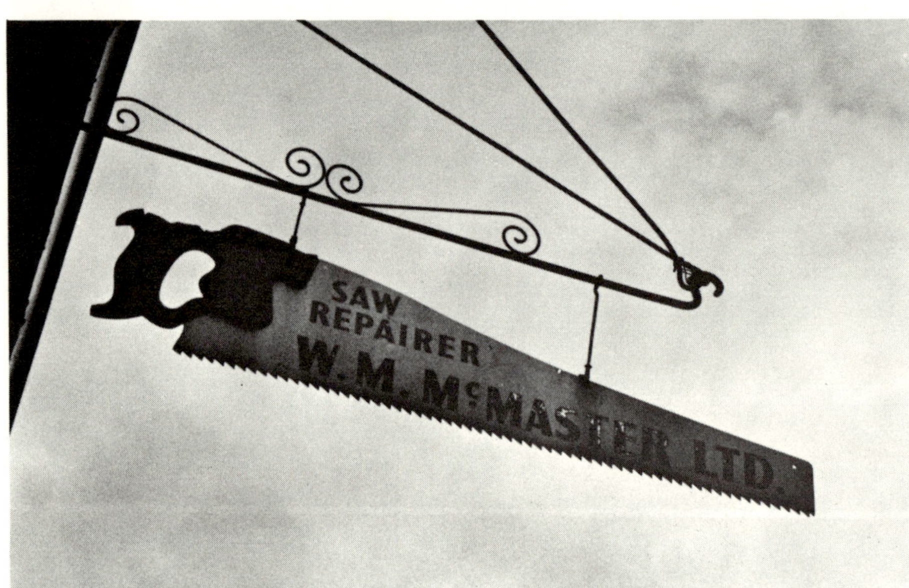

Trader's sign in Church Lane, 1960.

Tantra Barbus (real name William Scott), itinerant hardware merchant of the early 19th century.

that a similar sign, utilising a real saw, was to be seen above the door of a city centre shop until a few years ago. This custom also had its origin in the eighteenth century when some tradesmen found it more convenient, and in certain instances more appropriate, to feature a specimen of the merchandise outside their premises rather than a representative signboard.

Joy's Entry, scene of recent change: walls a few feet apart in distance, more than a century apart in time. Other modern innovations include 'no parking' lines in this reserve of the pedestrian.

The essential earthiness of the entries reflected the variety, character and interests of their population. This population, both resident and transitory, embraced a wide social scale; from the prominent merchant class through the small shop and stall-keepers to the casual labourers and finally those with no tangible means of support. These last, the unproductive flotsam of a largely indifferent society, had been a thorny problem from very early times, and it is to the credit of the already mentioned Charitable Society that it was eventually controllable, albeit within limits. There was yet another class of person who came into an altogether separate category. They might well be termed the 'professional beggar': able-bodied men who chose vagrancy as a way of life instead of having it thrust upon them through circumstances. They likewise had been a problem from an early date; as far back as 1680 the Sovereign had sanctioned a proposal 'That all Inmates and Beggars who came into and secretly conveyed themselves into ye Towne and beggs to releive beggars may be diligently sought after and a speedy course taken to discharge ye Towne of such'. This situation saw the emergence of an officially recognised, if locally unpopular, rank among these social outcasts. This was the 'bang beggar', who earned his keep by patrolling the streets and entries and compelling anyone discovered begging to deliver himself into the care of the poorhouse. Bang beggars were in reality little better than the riff-raff they lorded it over, but this 'set a thief to catch a thief' policy succeeded for a time, until the system came in for abuse when it was brought to the notice of the authorities that unscrupulous townsfolk were prepared to assume the role of a beggar and surrender themselves, temporarily of course, to the care of the Charitable Society in return for a bribe.

Pottinger's Entry, about 1900, photographed by Robert Welch.

Pottinger's Entry in 1972, loo ing from High Street towards Ann Street.

LOUNGE
THE MORNING
TO LET
OFFICE & STORAGE
ACCOMODATION
Macrory
Jefferson
HOP
LET

All in all, the scene in and about the entries must have been a colourful one, but it cannot have been conducive to a healthy existence. Conditions had been tolerable enough when the High Street and Ann Street group formed a kind of hollow square, with perhaps a scattering of well separated cottages within its boundaries, but as pressure on space increased the area soon became congested and, ultimately downright squalid. Stale air, stagnant cesspools, ash-heaps and other neglected refuse took a heavy toll on the stamina of the most resilient. The late J J Marshall once recounted a story of one entry resident who journeyed beyond the accustomed limits of his home territory and promptly fainted when he came into contact with fresh air. This tale, fanciful though it may be, could equally well have had its origin in fact. Not a few of the lower class lived out their lives in the cramped confines of these entries and courts, being either too lethargic or too poor, and in many cases too infirm, to raise themselves above a bare subsistence level.[2]

Pottinger's Court, c1900.

Eighteenth century housing in Pottinger's Court: mellowed brickwork and near-flush windows.

But the accumulated filth of the entries did not begin and end in these passageways. High Street itself was an equally insanitary place in the eighteenth century. The Farset River which flowed along its length and divided one side of the street from the other became a convenient receptacle for all kinds of effluence discarded by an unconcerned population. Ignorance bred apathy towards health hazards of this sort and although steps were taken from time to time to discourage, on pain of a fine, the abuse of public places in this manner, the streets of Belfast retained this stigma for many years.

BUILDING AND REDEVELOPMENT

The period from about 1767 to the end of the century saw considerable improvement in the rather down-at-heel state of building in Belfast, for it was then that new leases, providing for the first time reasonable security of tenure, were introduced by the fifth Earl of Donegall in a move to bring recognised standards to bear on the construction of all town houses and business premises.

The leases took the form of a printed indenture, with blank spaces reserved for entering individual terms and conditions. A typical example is that granted to Henry Joy in respect of tenements in Change Alley (later Joy's Entry) and High Street. It was 'for three lives, to continue for 99 years from 1 May 1767' at a yearly rent of £5, plus 2s duty.

Like a great many of those issued at the time, it was a repairing lease, and covered 'all that piece or Parcel of Ground, situate, lying and being on the East Side of Change Alley in the town of Belfast aforesaid, containing in Front next the said Street or Alley Seventy four feet be the same more or less and a small stable lying at a little distance being about thirty feet in length along said Alley ... also the front Shop in High Street'.

Winecellar Entry, 1840: focal point of the town's spirit trade.

Conditions of tenure varied from one to another, but by and large reflected the social status of the grantee. The more prominent the citizen the more stringent the terms, and no one was imposed on beyond his means. In a sense it brought to an end the long era of casual building; from then on the element of planned uniformity was evident in development within the town. Definite guidelines were carefully written into each indenture and in some cases went into minute detail. Valentine Jones, a well-known and respected merchant of the day, obtained a grant of building land at the High Street entrance to Winecellar Entry in 1780 and was instructed to 'Erect, Build and Finish

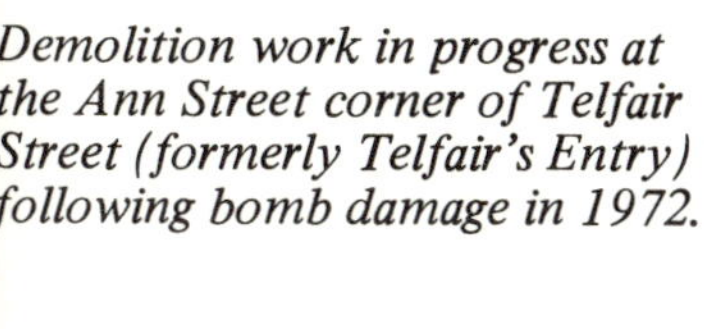

Demolition work in progress at the Ann Street corner of Telfair Street (formerly Telfair's Entry) following bomb damage in 1972.

... within two years ... in a good and Workmanlike Manner, and with good sound Materials ... two good and substantial Messuages or Tenements of Brick and Lime, three Stories high'. Other stipulations follow, including precise instructions as to wall thickness, timbers to be used, and, 'the Roof thereof to be well Slated'. The lease was for a term of 86 years at an annual rent of £18. Care was taken to ensure that the new premises would be maintained in a manner befitting the redeveloped town and the lessee in this instance was obliged to see that they would not be given over to any 'offensive Trade', such as, among others, slaughtering, tobacco-pipe burning, tallow-melting, or soap-boiling; these precautions secured for a time the residential status of the area before the process of industrialisation altered the whole concept of town dwelling.

Strict rules were applied to regulate the height of new buildings. High Street, at all times the prestigious thoroughfare, retained its architectural supremacy over secondary streets like Ann Street, while intervening lanes and entries were built to a discreet compromise. Representative of the period is a lease dated 20 July, 1767, wherein Montague Trimble is charged with rebuilding a tenement in Crown Entry with side walls 'Twenty eight feet high above the Surface of the Ground'.

Thus new houses and stores were built in the entries and older premises renovated, so that the area retained its primary commercial function. Merchants continued to reside in and around the entries, and from time to time dwelling-houses were advertised for sale or to be let in the columns of the *Belfast News Letter.* The following two examples may be regarded as typical:

> 'To be sold The Leasehold Interest of a Tenement in Pottinger's Entry, of which 24 years are unexpired from November next. There is on said Tenement a Dwelling-House, a Brew-House and cellar; as also a Store-House and Foundery, set for a Term of Years to solvent Tenants; and as the whole is now produces £20 per Year Profit Rent. For further Particulars enquire at Robert Laird, who lives in said House, and will treat for the same.
> Belfast, August 18th, 1768.'

> 'To be let and entered upon, from the first Day of November next, for such Term as may be agreed upon, three Dwelling-Houses, situate in the Crown Entry, Belfast. For further Particulars enquire at William Wallage, junr.
> Belfast, October 8th, 1772.'

Pottinger's Entry: from very early times an important commercial and residential centre. In Martin's Belfast Directory of 1840 it is the only 'entry' listed among 'the principal Streets of Business and Residence in Belfas At that time it housed the bindir rooms and general stationery warehouse of Marcus Ward.

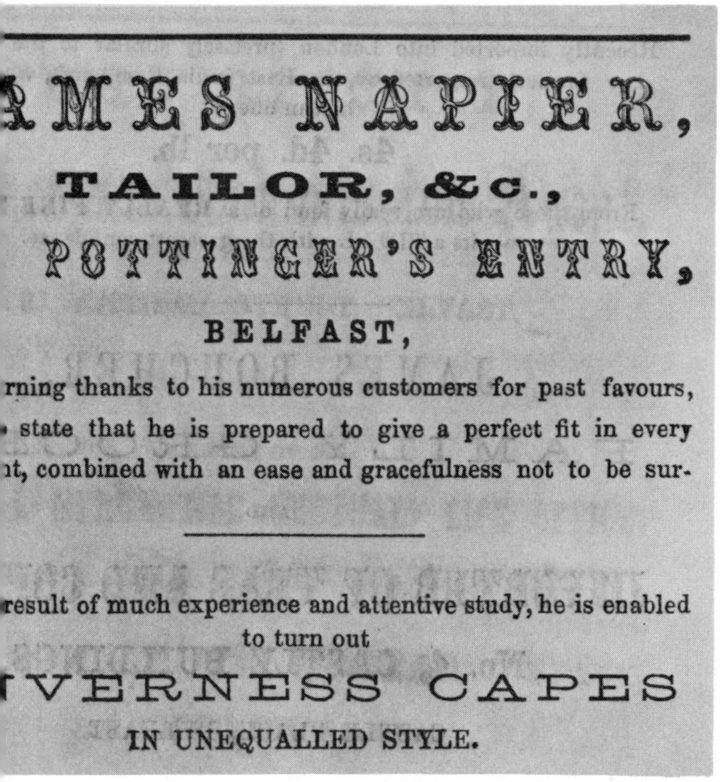

AMES NAPIER,
TAILOR, &c.,
POTTINGER'S ENTRY,
BELFAST,
rning thanks to his numerous customers for past favours,
state that he is prepared to give a perfect fit in every
it, combined with an ease and gracefulness not to be sur-
result of much experience and attentive study, he is enabled
to turn out
VERNESS CAPES
IN UNEQUALLED STYLE.

A typical business advertisement of 1872.

TO LET
OFFICE & STORAGE
ACCOMODATION
Macrory
Jefferson
44 DONEGALL STREET
Telephone BELFAST 21404
COPES
McCONNELL

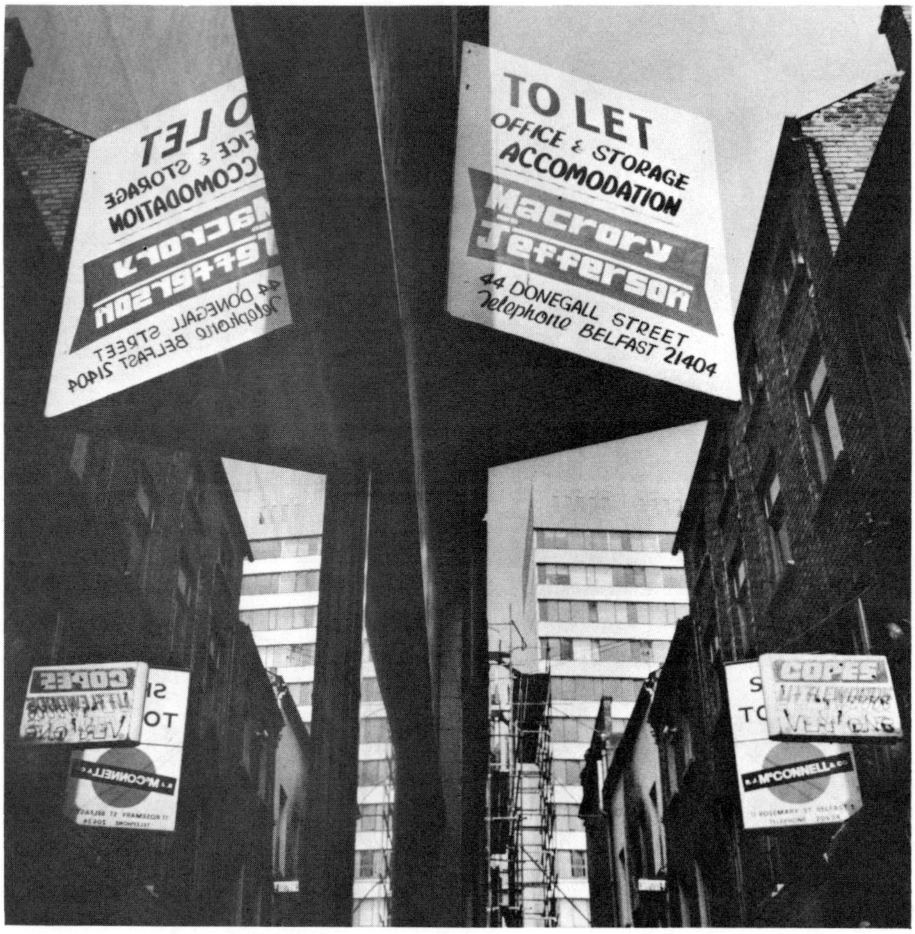

usiness accommodation to be
t in Pottinger's Entry in 1972.

By 1782, Belfast consisted of 2,026 houses and a population of 13,105. High on the list of trades represented in the town were the weavers - 389 in all - closely followed by the shoemakers with 224, and coopers, 163. Publicans numbered 119, or 'one to every 16th house', according to John Cough in *A Tour in Ireland.*

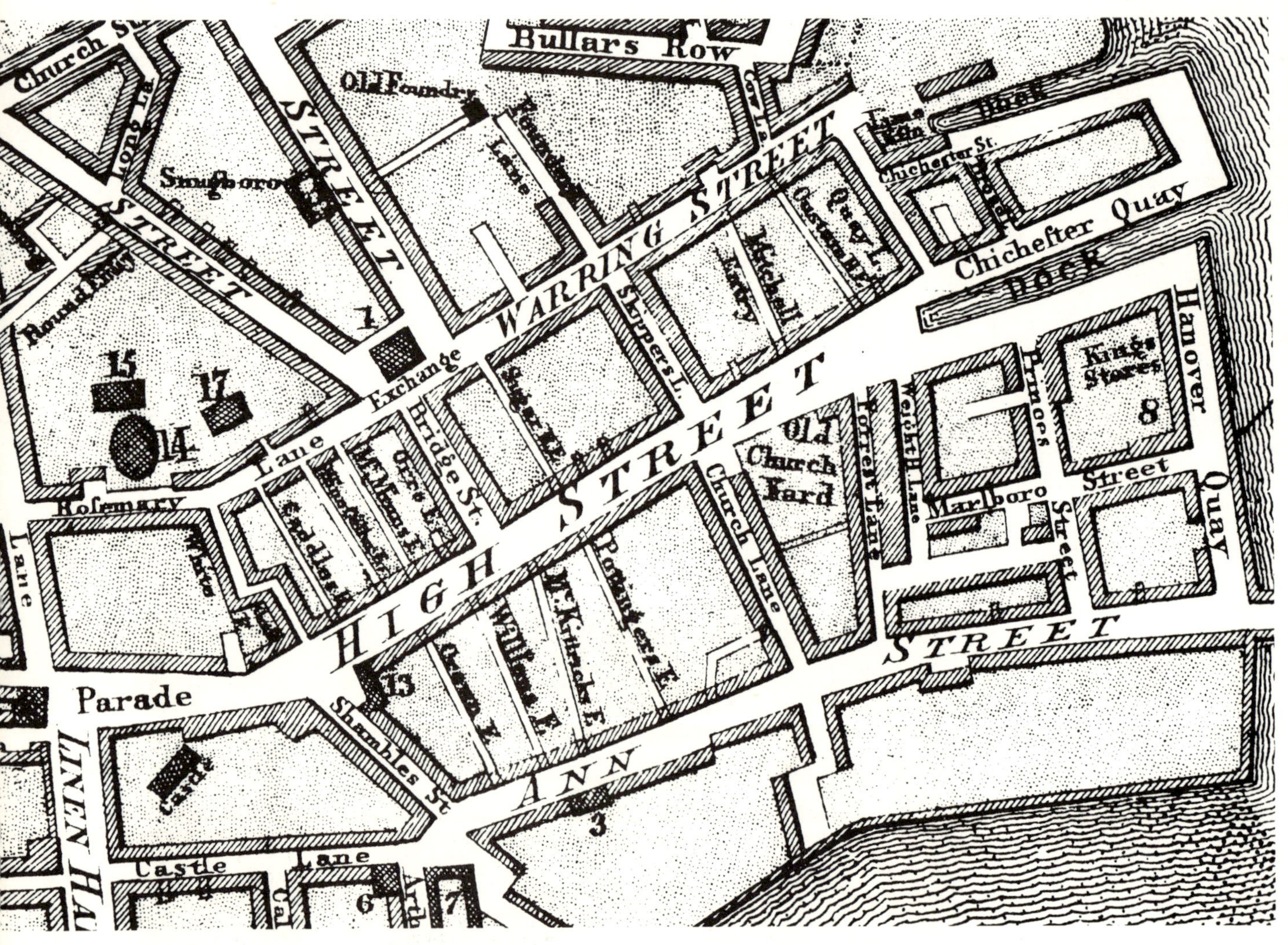

The High Street entries shown on a map of 1791, surveyed by James Williamson.

TURN OF THE CENTURY

The closing decades of the eighteenth century and the early years of the nineteenth century was an energetic and colourful period in the history of the High Street entries. Political issues apart, it was a time of great social activity. A state lottery scheme was then in vogue and attracted a deal of excitement. Not unlike our present-day Premium Bond draw, it offered handsome prizes ranging from (in 1768) two top prizes of £20,000 to numerous lesser ones of £20. The New Theatre in Ann Street, opened in 1778, provided a focal point for society-conscious gentry and their ladies and a welcome diversion for less well-to-do townsfolk. The streets were more crowded than ever before; 'water and milk-carriers, bakers' and butchers' baskets, bagmen with coals on their backs, sedan chairs, and wheelbarrows'; these and other tradesmen, as well as bell-men, watchmen and itinerant musicians, not to forget the inveterate beggar, all rubbed shoulders with merchant adventurers dispatching cargoes to far and often exotic destinations in their own ships.

Black Sam: one of many old-time street entertainers familiar to entry residents in the eighteenth and nineteenth centuries.

Pottinger's Entry, 1890s, looking towards High Street. Note enclosed entrance (removed early in the present century) similar to that at the Ann Street approach.

Crown Entry: enclosed midway section.

As the new century advanced, provincial towns became more easy of access to the traveller with the establishment of regular and dependable coach services. The ticket office for the Fair trader Day Coach for Armagh and the Phoenix Day Coach for Lurgan was at No 1 Crown Entry.

Most people went about their business on foot; hence, presumably, the high incidence of shoemakers in the town at that time. For the wealthy or the infirm, or those bent on purely social pursuits, the alternative to walking was the sedan chair. A number of chair bearers lived in the entries, ready for business day and night. Thomas Gaffikin recorded that, in the early nineteenth century, 'the sedan chairs were kept in the entries off High Street, and the measured tramp of the bearers could be heard going to and from the theatre, evening parties, or to the church on Sundays'. With some of the entries barely six feet wide and stacked in places with barrels, bales of cotton, sacks of sugar and like merchandise, movement must have been restricted enough for pedestrians, let alone cumbersome sedan chairs - especially so at night when badly maintained and hopelessly ineffectual oil lamps did little to illuminate the shadowy corners. As a general rule, sedan chairs were equipped with their own individual lamps to light the way for the bearers as they negotiated these uneven passageways after dark.

Sedan chair, early nineteenth century. (From a painting by Frank McKelvey)

Wilson's Court.

Sedan chairs saw a long and useful life in Belfast. They survived the introduction of hackney cars and, surprisingly, were still in service when that most revolutionary mode of travel, the railway, brought distant settlements within easy reach of the expanding town. Uneven and muddy streets prolonged the era of the sedan chair, as wheeled transport was scarcely practical or comfortable for short journeys. A fare of 9d was charged for 'a set down within the lights' up to midnight, increasing to 1s 3d thereafter. Waiting time was charged at 6d for each quarter of an hour. The last remaining sedan establishment was operated by Dennis Kane from 16 Joy's Entry in the early 1840s.

Street musicians of yesterday and today: updated but essentially alike.

Although some improvement had been effected in the condition of the streets from the state of things a century before, attention was lacking in fundamental matters such as, for example, drainage, and some of the entries were liable to flooding during a spring tide.[3] But such considerations were secondary to the great commercial incentive in the air, and if wealth was unevenly distributed it was at least seen to be at work. In 1842 Thackeray visited Belfast in the course of his Irish tour and noted that 'Many of the merchants' counting-houses are crowded in little old-fashioned "entries", or courts, such as one sees about the Bank in London. In and about these, and in the principal streets in the daytime, is a great activity, and homely unpretending bustle.' His allusion to the entries being old-fashioned, even then, indicates their early maturity.

A healthy economy was now evident; thrift and sound business acumen were becoming hallmarks of the Belfast merchants and there was an atmosphere of urgency in the streets, a desire to get on with the job: 'The men have a business look,' observed Thackeray, 'and one sees very few flaunting dandies, as in Dublin.' It was, as Gaffikin pointed out, 'at that time an honour to be known as a Belfast merchant.' This entirely purposeful attitude to business persisted and might be said to be equally characteristic today.

From a practical point of view the transformation resulting from the new leases granted in the latter half of the eighteenth century must have been considerable. Even in the less important entries houses of two stories were normal:

> 'HOUSES TO LET: IN BLUE-BELL ENTRY
> That HOUSE, No 7, two stories high, would be let low to
> a good tenant.' (*Belfast News Letter,* 15 January, 1819)

High Street in the first half of the nineteenth century: 'airy, wide, and of imposing aspect'.

Thatch roofs were going out of use on all but the most lowly houses and were in any case banned within the town before the middle of the nineteenth century. By that time most of the buildings fronting onto High Street and Ann Street were of three stories, brick built, and had roofs of imported slate. James Adair Pilson, writing in 1846, was obviously impressed with the prospect of High Street. It was 'airy, wide, and of imposing aspect, and makes amends, by the magnificence of its shops and warehouses, and by its clean and cheerful appearance, together with the enlivening excitement caused by a perfect whirl of business, for some irregularity in its alignment and architectural structure.'

rown Entry and the changes of a decade:
n 1962 (left), and 1972 (right).

The general valuations carried out in the 1830s set out clearly the dimensions of buildings in the town and provide a useful comparison between those of the principal and lesser thoroughfares. The tallest buildings in High Street reached 47 ft, with average heights in the region of 35 ft; while in Ann Street no building exceeded 39 ft. Buildings in the intervening entries observed the niceties demanded by convention and graded their heights accordingly. Of the sixteen houses in Crown Entry, the tallest (significantly at the High Street end) reached 32 ft. Others in this group were: 30 ft (four houses), 26 ft (four houses), 23 ft 6 in (two houses), 20 ft (one house), 17 ft (two houses), 15 ft (one house), and

13 ft 6 in (one house). The tallest building located in any of the High Street to Ann Street entries was No 1 Pottinger's Entry, at 38 ft 6 in.

At that time No 1 was a warehouse, but, as had been the case with many similar premises, it had originally been a private dwelling-house and was now adapted to merchandising requirements. No one entry can be singled out as being wholly representative of the business and private life contained in these secondary streets in the nineteenth century, such was the infinite variety of trades carried on; but as a convenient example Pottinger's Entry was not untypical. In 1840 it had four tailors, two stationers, two merchants, a publican, printer and flesher, and three private residences. Nearby entries boasted such trades and professions as

Pottinger's Entry in the nineteenth century, from a painting by E. Hanford.

shoemakers, sweeps, hackney-car proprietors, watchmen, schoolmasters, messengers, joiners, confectioners, coopers, cabinet-makers, writing clerks, butchers, and many more besides. In the Belfast *Directory* of 1840 several addresses in the entries bear the intriguing classification 'entertainment' immediately after the name of the householder.

orner tenement in Joy's Entry: ignified and, at one time, desirable.

Lodging-houses were abundant, but there was a noticeable decline in the number of private residences in the High Street entries in the nineteenth century. It was symptomatic of a sociological change that had been overtaking this part of the old town for many years. It was no longer a fashionable area with wealthy merchants who were looking to more distinguished surroundings, such as the focal point provided by the opulent White Linen Hall, erected in 1783. On the borders of this and along Linen Hall Street elegant terraces were built to satisfy the expensive tastes of a new generation of speculators attuned to an era of industrial expansion.

At the same time, a great many working class townspeople held on to small, clustered tenements in the entries, particularly those on the north side of High Street. In 1840, nine houses in Graham's Entry were occupied by yearly tenants paying rents of between £2 6s 2d and £12. But conditions close to the centre of the old town were not nearly so bad as in some of the peripheral entries noticed by O'Hanlon in the 1850s: Hudson's Entry, 'a complete den of vice and uncleanness, probably unsurpassed in what is called the civilised world'; and Round Entry, 'a place celebrated for its iniquity'. Poverty, overcrowding and appalling sanitation were all present to some extent in the entries and back lanes of Belfast in the nineteenth century, though it is evident that those belonging to the High Street and Ann Street group were less affected by these pressures. Perhaps this was because they had succeeded in maintaining a balance between residential and commercial properties from an early date, and also because they remained accessible to, and frequented by, the public and the town authorities at all times.

NAME ORIGINS

Exactly when the word 'entry' came into use with regard to these streets is not known. They are clearly defined as entries on maps and leases of the latter half of the eighteenth century and were probably designated as such when houses and offices were first built over their narrow entrances (clauses entitling lessees to 'build over' are to be found in several of the 1767 Donegall estate leases). Passageways thus enclosed would have been self-suggestive of the title 'entry', though the distinction between an entry and, say, a lane or alley, must remain a subtle one – if, indeed, the designation is other than fortuitous. It may, however, be pertinent to note that MacLanachan's map of 1715 suffixes the words 'alley' and 'lane' to the names of these passages at a time when they were still relatively sparsely developed.

The actual naming of the individual entries followed no particular pattern and if they differed at all in their nomenclature from that of the more important streets of the town it was simply that they acquired names to a greater extent through association, rather than having them given. As the entries evolved from accesses to private dwellings and business premises in the first instance, to become accepted public rights of way and, later in their development, significant thoroughfares, so they attracted identifying names, initially from local people and after a time from the authorities. It is likely that in the early days the entries were known by name only to the inhabitants and to those having business dealings there, as street nameplates were not statutory until after 1800. As these names were subject to change from time to time this would account for variations that occur on contemporary maps and plans. Some entries may not have received their 'official' names until the first Ordnance Survey was carried out in 1832.

Business court at 53 High Street (Granville Buildings): typical of the many small, semi-private entrances to dwellings and commercial premises in this area in the nineteenth century and before.

More often than not we find personalities of the day recalled in the naming of entries: Pottinger, Hamilton, Wilson, Joy, Telfair; these, very representative of the merchant profession, are in existence today, while numerous others – Caddell, Quin, Clugston, Mitchell, etc – have long since been obliterated by war and development. Some entries were associated with a particular trade or industry and were given names accordingly: Sugarhouse Entry, Winecellar Entry, Weigh-house Lane, Sweeps Entry. Others, less readily definable, had names whose origin can only be conjectured, such as the romantic-sounding Bluebell Entry and the adjoining Elbow Lane, though several possibilities come readily to mind. Crown Entry, it is generally believed, was so called in deference to the first Custom House in the town, built on or about this site in the seventeenth century.

A number of entries changed their status in the course of their history – Telfair's Entry is now Telfair Street, for instance – while others changed their names completely as new occupiers succeeded older families and imposed their influence on the locality. Clugston's Entry of the eighteenth century had become Legg's Lane in the nineteenth; Joy's Entry was earlier called Change Alley as well as McKitterick's Entry; Winecellar Entry was originally Bigart's Alley and was also known as Customhouse Lane. There are other examples, but these will suffice to show how later generations, changing fashions, and the spirit of the times left their bold imprint on these little streets during Belfast's formative years.[4]

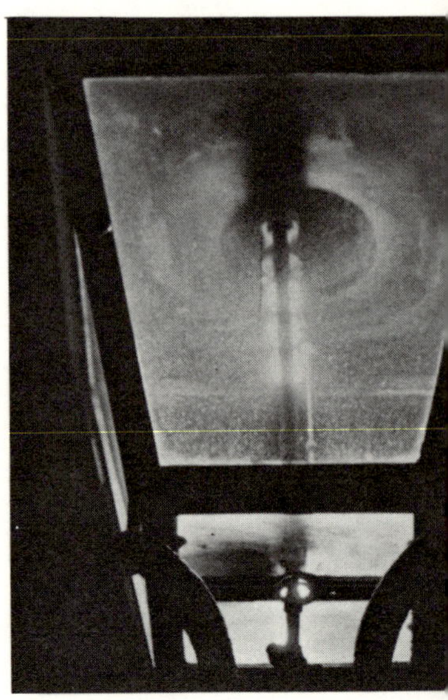

STREET LIGHTING

Belfast in the eighteenth century must have been a dark and dismal place at night. Apart from the pallid glow of candlelight from the windows of private houses (a statutory obligation on the population of certain districts at one time) the streets of the old town were beset with hazards of one sort or another for the unwary traveller. In 1761 the matter was given serious consideration for the first time and a lamplighter appointed to

Crown Entry

Pottinger's Entry after dark, photographed in 1962.

take charge of the proposed new oil lamps to be positioned at strategic points along the streets. But few lamps were actually erected, mainly because there was a shortage of public money for the project, and the population continued to stumble about in the darkness. In 1768 the *Belfast News Letter* reported that 'Carmen leave their cars in public places at night, whereby people fall over them breaking their legs or arms. Penalty for so doing 10/-'.

The first purposeful steps were taken in 1800 when an Act was introduced for 'Paving, Cleaning, Lighting and improving the several Streets, Squares, Lanes and Passages within the town of Belfast'. Progress must have been fairly rapid, as on 11 August 1801 the *Belfast News Letter* published a tender for the painting, maintenance and repairing of 400 public lamps in the town. Severe penalties, extending to public whipping and in extreme cases transportation, were imposed on vandalism. Ten years later, in 1811, the Police Committee had charge of 700 lamps. Lighting and maintenance was still contracted out, though the Committee made fine quality burning oil available to the contractor at £35 per ton (12 tons were judged necessary to keep the lamps of Belfast alight throughout the winter months). Alternatively, the contractor could buy his supply of oil direct from a merchant at the lowest market price he could find.

Gas lamps used in the High Street and Ann Street entries: The familiar Scots lantern type (left) was constructed locally from standard parts available in Britain. It has a three-mantle burner and was wall-mounted in the entries (with the permission of property owners) instead of on the usual but cumbersome pillar. Also adapted to wall-mounting was the swan-neck suspension lamp (right) which provided a more efficient light source with either five or six mantles (up to twelve were used in main street versions).

But if the number of lamps increased, so also did the vandalism. In one week of 1811, for example, 49 public lamps were broken, and a reward of £20 failed to bring the perpetrators to book. Often, however, the greatest problem lay with the lamps themselves and they required constant attention – which they seldom received – to maintain even a moderate level of efficiency. For this reason the entries were not the safest places after dark and many who steered a shaky course through the letter of the law lurked in their gloomy corners and courts. Merchants and tradesmen were wary of carrying large sums of money on their person, while unescorted ladies were equally well advised, for more delicate reasons, to avoid these secretive streets. In 1817 Sugarhouse Entry was banned to sedan chairs carrying female passengers after midnight; though just why that hour should be selected as the watershed of moral conduct is not revealed.

But help was at hand for the virtuous citizen. The era of oil lighting was mercifully a short one and in 1823 gas was introduced and soon took over completely as the illuminant of public places. By its light all was distinguishable and 'each man could recognise his neighbour'.

NEWSPAPERS AND PRINTING

The entries were the source of a great deal of the literary outpourings of the late eighteenth and early nineteenth century in Belfast. Stirring times and events demanded suitable vehicles in which viewpoints of the day could be brought squarely to the notice of the public. In January 1792, the *Northern Star* began its six years' existence from an office in Wilson's Court under the editorship of Samuel Neilson. It was ably supported by such forceful writers as, among others, Thomas Russell and William Steel Dickson – names that were to be on many lips before the century reached its stormy close – and it also attracted pertinent comment from the ordinary citizen concerned for the outcome of political issues:

Northern Star.

THE PUBLIC WILL OUR GUIDE — THE PUBLIC GOOD OUR END

MBER 435.] FROM MONDAY, FEBRUARY 29, TO THURSDAY, MARCH 3, 1796. [PRICE TWO-PENCE HALFPENNY

Put the following paragraph in your paper, and let me see the man vho dare blink at it:

Necessity as well as nature, shews, that monarchy is the most complete and perfect form of government, and experience proves t it will continue so, if under the direction of the people. The epresentative system, is, of all others, most likely to secure human elicity, but to do so, it must be guarded by the wise and necessary heck of

ABSOLUTE MONARCHY!

All theory in government ought to be exploded, because government s a practical thing.

Let no man imagine, that any executive government can possibly be iseful, unless founded on theory. Men who are wise, and have no ixed or unchangeable principles, but must wait, and waver, and remble, and laugh, and cry, and say nothing.

JIMMY M'CLAVER.'

The *Star* emerged as a champion of the volunteer movement and acquired a measure of notoriety which ended with its closure in 1797 by a detachment of militia who broke up the formes of type and disabled the presses. The voice of independent thought that had characterised the *Northern Star* was reborn to some extent in the *Irishman* newspaper, issued from No 2 Pottinger's Entry between 1819 and 1826. It had a redoubtable and fair-minded editor in John Lawless – 'honest Jack Lawless', as he came to be called by the citizens of Belfast.

Crown Entry, looking towards the Ann Street entrance. The Vindicator publishing office occupied the position of the present Capstan Lounge, to the left of the picture.

Crown Entry from Ann Street, drawn by Raymond Piper in 1952. It is an entry of many evocative associations with the old town; it housed the Crown Tavern, in which the Belfast Chamber of Commerce (formed in 1783) held its council meetings 'on every Thursday Evening precisely at seven o'clock', and in which the Society of United Irishmen was inaugurated in 1791.

Read memorial, Friar's Bush burial ground, Stranmillis.

The needs of commerce were served by the *Belfast Commercial Chronicle,* first published in 1805 from Wilson's Court; it appeared three times weekly, on Monday, Wednesday and Saturday. In 1853, two enterprising brothers, Robert and Daniel Read, set up a publishing office in Crown Entry from which they issued the *Morning News,* now extant in the *Irish News.* And the *Belfast News Letter,* one of the oldest surviving newspapers in the British Isles (founded 1737), and one which provides the historian with valuable glimpses of everyday life in eighteenth-century Belfast, was printed for a time in a little court off Joy's Entry.

A mid-nineteenth century advertisement for a printing house.

Two other nineteenth century newspapers had their offices in the entries: the *Vindicator,* founded in 1839, was published from premises at the corner of Crown Entry and Ann Street; and the *Belfast Mercury* (1851) was based in Winecellar Entry, in the court facing the front entrance of White's Tavern. It is not surprising, nor is it coincidental, that these publications had their offices located in the High Street and Ann Street entries. As with many another flourishing business of the day, the printed word had quickly assumed an intrinsic role in the affairs of the town, and the machinery from which the news emanated was necessarily to be found at the very centre of events. Newspapers were avidly read, especially by merchants and shopkeepers, though not everyone purchased a copy: 'It was the custom fifty years ago for the newspapers to be carried about and left at the houses and offices for an hour's reading on payment of one penny', wrote Gaffikin in 1875. Tavern proprietors took care to ensure that an up-to-date supply of local newspapers and periodicals was on hand for the convenience of their more important customers.

The conveyance of newspapers to outlying districts was often entrusted to an independent carrier and, as there was little finance available for this side of the business, publishers found difficulty in finding reliable men to undertake the job:

'A careful, sober Man is wanted, to carry this Paper from Belfast to Larne, by Carrickfergus - none need apply without proper recommendations.' (*Northern Star*, 29 September 1792)

Jobbing printers and engravers also favoured the entries for their businesses. The printing trade was actively supported by the tradespeople of the town, and the appetite of the public for broadsheets and popular ballads of the times kept the presses busy. In 1840 there were letterpress printing establishments in Joy's Entry, Pottinger's Entry and Crown Entry; and copperplate printers in Hamilton's Court.

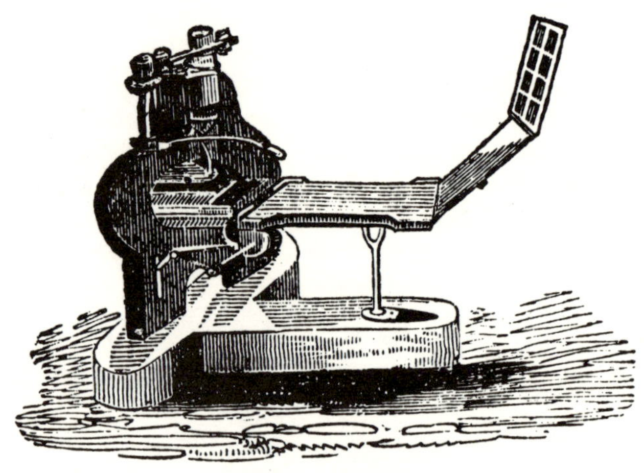

GENERAL

PRINTING ESTABLISHMENT,

JOY'S ENTRY

(*Opposite Bridge-st.*),

Belfast.

PAUL KELSO

Respectfully informs his Friends and the Public, that every description of

JOB PRINTING AND BOOK WORK,

Is carefully executed by him in the above Old Established Concern.

He trusts, by giving strict attention to all Orders with which he may be favoured, to merit a share of public support.

2 A

A mid-nineteenth century advertisement for a printing house.

ENTRY SCHOOLS

Many of the Belfast's early schools took root in the High Street entries. Usually they were small privately owned and administered concerns with a limited clientele. Classes were conducted in the home of the teacher, since the limited money available did not extend to providing separate accommodation. One such schoolroom, held in a house in Joy's Entry in the 1830s by John Gillespie, measured 6ft 6in by 17ft. But if the schools were small they were also prolific and bore a certain likeness to the 'hedge schools' that thrived in country districts in the early nineteenth century. Doubtless the entry schools were a cut above their rural counterparts, and some indeed made a tangible contribution to the educational needs of generations of children otherwise deprived of facilities.

Notable in this respect was the progressive, not to say unique, school inaugurated by David Manson in his house in Clugston's Entry in 1755. A glimpse of its advanced educational policy is contained in the wording of his opening announcement - namely, teaching 'by way of amusement'. Manson regarded boredom and fear of punishment as inhibitory to successful instruction and in place of the accustomed 'discipline of the rod' he substituted a system of teaching by reward. His success was such that the school soon outgrew his modest entry house and he

Ordnance Survey map of 1858, showing site of Legg's Lane, formerly Clugston's Entry. Legg's Lane and the adjacent Caddell's Entry were demolished in 1865 to make way for the proposed new thoroughfare of Lombard Street. The map also indicates the site of the Daily Mercury office in Winecellar Entry.

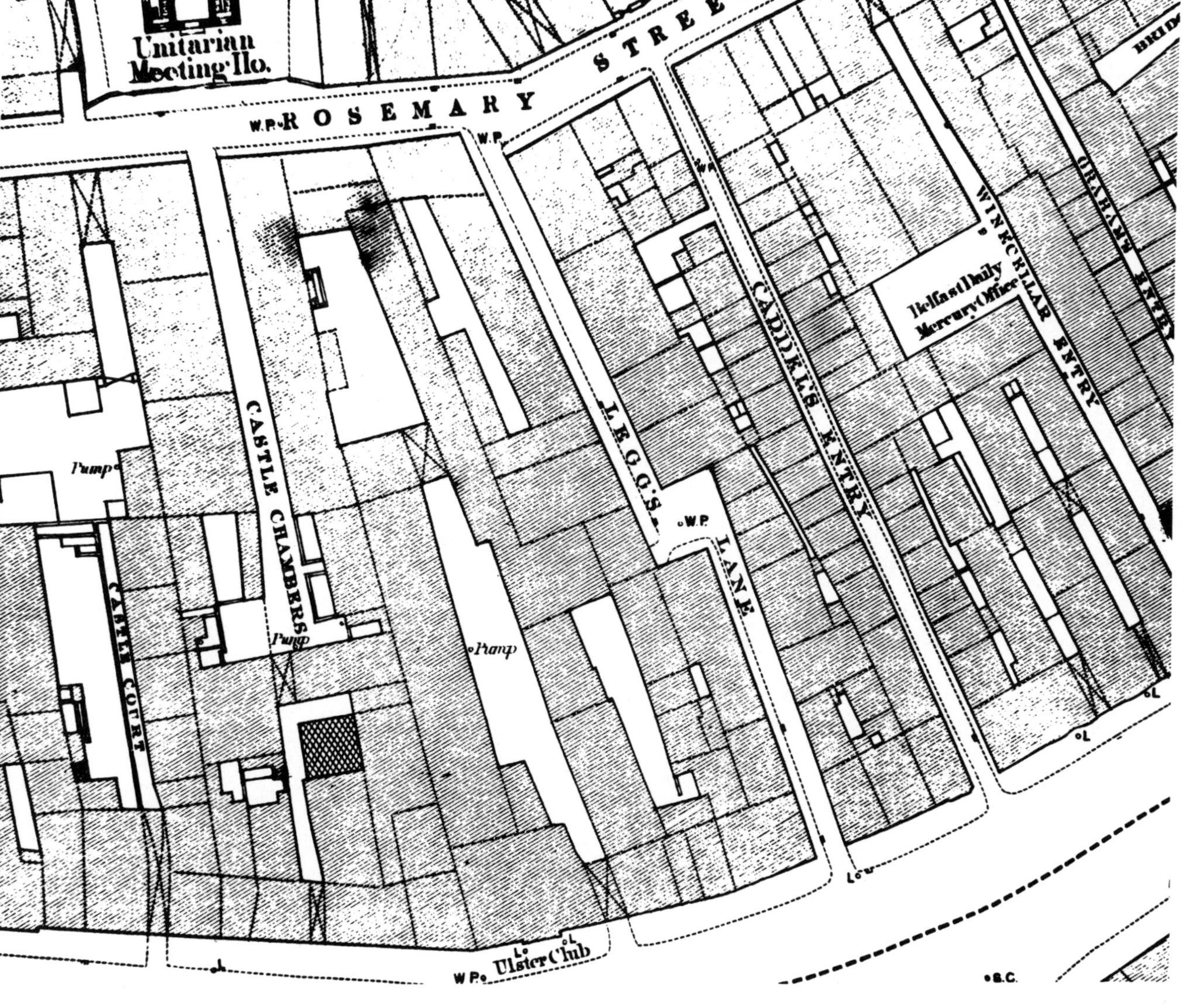

MR. PERCY'S SCHOOL,

In that neat and commodious well-lighted House, supplied with the purest Pipe-water, &c.

NO. 1, POTTINGER'S-ENTRY,

To be Opened on MONDAY the 26th October inst.—No Entrance required, nor any Pay to commence till 1st November.

W. PERCY, who has been chiefly employed, both as a Public and Private Teacher, for more than 20 years (from the age of 15), and can produce a great number of the most respectable *Testimonials*, of *Ability* and *past Services*, wishing to *establish* himself as a Teacher in the TOWN of BELFAST, on *Moderate Terms*, within the reach of the Children of those truly *respectable* Classes, *Dealing and Mechanical Men*, he therefore will open School at the above-mentioned place and time, where he will teach as follows, viz.:—

MORNING-SCHOOL, from 8 till 10 in Winter, and from 7 till 9 in Summer; exclusively devoted to Syllables, Dictionary, and Grammar—for Syllables, 2*s*. 2*d*.—Dictionary, 3*s*. 3*d*.—Grammar, 4*s*. 4*d*. per Quarter.

DAY-SCHOOL, from 10 A. M. till 3 P. M.—Rudiments of Spelling and Reading, 5*s*. 5*d*.—Ditto, with Writing, 6*s*. 6*d*.—With Arithmetic, 1st Class, 7*s*. 7*d*. (as far as Fractions)—2d Class, 8*s*. 8*d*. per Quarter.

EVENING-SCHOOL, from 4 till 6—Writing, 3*s*. 3*d*.—Arithmetic, 4*s*. 4*d*. per Quarter.

NIGHT-SCHOOL, from 7 till 9, the same.

☞ For any number of *Evenings* or *Nights* less than the whole—Writing ¾*d*. and Arithmetic 1*d*. *per Night*.

N. B. Book-keeping, Navigation, Mensuration, Geography, with minute reference to Maps, the *Practical Use of the Globes*, taught on moderate Terms—the Money to be paid *in advance*, proportioned to the degree of Knowledge wished to be communicated, or Problems to be demonstrated.

*** Wishing to pay a very particular attention to *Elocution*, he will deliver a great variety of *Specimens*, on the Evening of the day of commencement—to begin precisely at 7 o'Clock.—Admittance: Gentlemen, 10*d*.; Ladies, and Youths below 16 years, 5*d*.

Prospec for Wil Percy's School, opened 1 Potti Entry i 1807. I enticem of pipe water a congen conditi

transferred to High Street and subsequently to another residence with an adjoining schoolroom in Rosemary Lane. 1768 once again found him in the process of moving to still larger premises, this time in Donegall Street. Manson's reputation outlived his schools. He himself was far ahead of his time with his enlightened approach to education, the principles of which were to be carried on long after his death in 1792.

Mention must be made also of the school opened by James Sheridan Knowles in Crown Entry in 1811. Knowles was something of an enigmatic figure. He settled in the town of Belfast early in the nineteenth century, having come with his father from county Cork, and for a time pursued a career as an actor before turning to teaching elocution as a means of livelihood. But his inherent artistic temperament was ill-suited to the disciplines of the teaching profession (his father, indeed, was dismissed from his post as headmaster of the Academical Institution on similar grounds). Eventually Sheridan found his niche as a playwright; his drama *Caius Gracchus* was staged at Belfast's Theatre Royal to much acclaim in 1815, and five years later London audiences were to turn out in large numbers to attend his *Virginius* at Covent Garden.

James Sheridan Knowles, playwright and teacher, 1784–1862.

PUBLIC HOUSES

From a very early date Belfast's inns and taverns were located in the entries, these enclosed streets providing the gregarious conditions on which they prospered. Amid the general camaraderie of the eighteenth-century town, public houses mushroomed practically in every street, and not a few gained renown of one kind or another in later years. O'Hanlon was scathing in his criticism of these establishments in the mid-nineteenth century, citing their frequency as one of the main causes of the human degradation he encountered among the lower classes. But Gaffikin, writing of much the same period, takes a kindlier view and points to the homeliness of many of the taverns in and about these old byways. He recalled that the most popular eating and drinking places were those away from the main thoroughfares and gave as examples: Mrs Stewart's in Crown Entry, Mrs M'Alister's in Graham's Entry and Sheal's in Wilson's Court.

Sugarhouse Entry, late nineteenth century.

Dining out was not the prerogative of the gentry; good evening dinners accompanied by strong rum and heady wines were cheap by London standards (Thackeray reckoned that half-crown meal in Belfast was equivalent to a seven shilling one in the English capital), and the amount of local competition succeeded in keeping prices keen. Bradshaw's first *General and Commercial Directory* of 1819 recorded some fifteen public houses in the High Street entries alone, and five of these had two public houses in each: Pottinger's Entry, Crown Entry, Legg's Lane, Bluebell Entry and Caddell's Entry. Interesting, if not unusual for the time, was the high percentage of women who owned and managed taverns, including one who laboured under the redoubtable name of Jane M'Grotty. The famous Peggy Barclay had removed

Advertisement in the Belfast Commercial Chronicle of 25 May, 1811, for Haylock's Tavern. This was the former Dr Franklin Tavern owned by Peggy Barclay. Typical of many similar establishments of the day, it carried a wide range of food-stuffs and dealt in ships' supplies. In later years the tavern was acquired by Abraham Bambridge and it continued to be known as the 'Bambridge' for almost a century (see previous picture).

HAYLOCK'S TAVERN,

SUGAR-HOUSE-ENTRY.

THE Public are respectfully informed, that the Tavern in Sugar-House-entry, formerly occupied by Mrs. BARKLEY, is now opened by T. HAYLOCK, for the accommodation of the Public, in a manner that he hopes will give general satisfaction.—Soups, Dinners, and Suppers prepared and served up on the shortest Notice—Hams and Spiced Beef by the Pound, or entire Pieces—Fowls, Chickens, &c. in readiness for Ships' use; and a Stock of the very best Wines, Spirits, Malt Liquors, Cyder, Perry, &c. &c.

970) May 22.

N. B. The NEWSPAPERS are taken in at this House.

from the scene by 1819. Her tavern, the Dr Franklin, had on earlier occasions played host to the society of United Irishmen, but the notoriety of that association had caused her to seek quieter employment in an out of town public house. Her old tavern in Sugarhouse Entry,[5] with its famed oyster suppers and reputation for congeniality, passed through the hands of many proprietors and served an appreciative public until comparatively modern times.

WALKER'S

OYSTER ROOMS,

3, WINECELLAR ENTRY, BELFAST,

J. W. respectfully announces to his numerous Customers and Friends that he has a constant supply daily of CARRICKFERGUS, CARLINGFORD, REDBANK, and GREENCASTLE, and all other kinds of OYSTERS.

All Orders punctually attended to.

Advertisements of 1872, representative of the several taverns in the High Street entries a century ago.

CROWN SHELL FISH TAVERN,

11, CROWN ENTRY, BELFAST,

(NEXT DOOR TO THE "MORNING NEWS" OFFICE),

THOMAS KANE, Proprietor.

The Oyster House in connexion with this Tavern is always regularly supplied with Oysters, Lobsters, and other Shell Fish in their season, always fresh, and of the choicest quality.

Every attention is given to the comfort and convenience of Customers and Visitors.

Country Orders punctually attended to.

Even in the 1800s, many taverns had come and gone. In 1792 the Porterhouse in Sugarhouse Entry was let as a private residence, while an advertisement in the *Belfast News Letter* of 20 January, 1801, announced the leasing of 'A Dwelling-House in Legg's Lane, formerly the White-Cross Inn, but lately occupied by a genteel family gone to London...' The White-Cross Inn must have been restored to its former function for it was certainly known as such when the Belfast Harp Society held its inaugural meeting in one of its rooms in 1808. The old Crown Tavern seems to have disappeared by the early nineteenth century, as had other less notable public houses in the course of rebuilding.

It is of passing interest, but worth recording, that in 1972 the High Street entries supported a total of six public houses. None – with the possible exception of the Morning Star in Pottinger's Entry – really fosters an atmosphere of times past, though White's Tavern in Winecellar Entry makes pretensions to do so, albeit in an overtly artificial fashion. Of the remainder the best that can be said is that they are functional and, within limits, not unpleasant.

Winecellar Entry at the end of the nineteenth century and in 1972.

THEATRICAL ASSOCIATIONS

In 1843, Thackeray noted that 'the fine arts do not appear as yet to flourish in Belfast'. Certainly the Belfast of the eighteenth and nineteenth century lacked much of the cultural finesse of Dublin, a situation that was partly attributable, as we have already seen, to the town's preoccupation with commerce. But if Belfast was dilatory in such matters it was not entirely neglectful, and while no great aesthetic attached to the early town there were nevertheless occasional successes and odd moments of individual achievement in the arts to allay later charges that it was 'a cultural desert'.

Brief reference may be made here to the old Vaults theatre in Ann Street, for it has close associations with our subject. Its existence is first recorded in the 1750s and it was almost certainly the earliest permanent playhouse in the town. From its stage Belfast audiences had their first taste of Shakespearean drama – as well as less edifying pastiches of a more raucous kind. Typical of the time was a production of 1766, promoted as 'A New Ballad Farce called The Honours of Belfast', by an unnamed local Gentleman. It had not, claimed the advertisement, perhaps unnecessarily, been performed anywhere else before. The Vaults appears to have stood on the north side of Ann Street (reputedly between Crown Entry and Wilson's Court) and drew a great deal of support

from the population of the adjoining entries, while visiting players attached to travelling companies found convenient lodgings in these streets.

The entries have other theatrical connections. Cole's Alley, the narrow right-angled passage linking Ann Street with Church Lane, is said to have numbered Harriet Mellon among its inhabitants. Miss Mellon appeared on the stage of the Ann Street Theatre in the early years of her career and was afterwards elevated to the glittering ranks of London society when she married the Duke of St Albans. No actual record of her house in Cole's Alley exists, if indeed her occupation of it is founded on anything other than hearsay; but tradition, always susceptible to the romantic, is to be forgiven if it chooses to couple her rags-to-riches story with such humble beginnings.

If Harriet Mellon's Belfast residence remains a matter of some doubt, that of dramatist and teacher James Sheridan Knowles is known with reasonable certainty. He lived in Crown Entry, at, states Benn, 'the first door to the right on passing into the entry from High Street'.

Turning to more modern times, that splendid paean to the Victorian era, the Empire Theatre, might claim a peripheral connection with our story as its stage doors opened into Telfair's Entry. But the Empire is of course gone, having been demolished in the 1960s; while Telfair's Entry, now substantially rebuilt and earmarked for further development, exists as Telfair Street.

Empire Theatre: demolition, October 1962.

Telfair Street (drawn by Raymond Piper in 1951) was formerly Telfair's Entry, named after Robert Telfair, a prominent merchant of the early nineteenth century. The Telfair Tobacco factory was situated here.

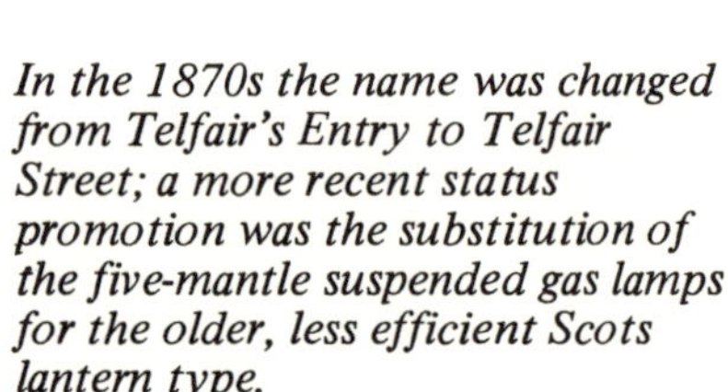

In the 1870s the name was changed from Telfair's Entry to Telfair Street; a more recent status promotion was the substitution of the five-mantle suspended gas lamps for the older, less efficient Scots lantern type.

VICTORIANA

If it was the commercial and social life of the town which gave the entries their inherent character in the first instance, it was the decorative hardware of the Victorian age which completed the embellishment. The Victorian influence has survived more flamboyantly in places other than the entries, possibly because much of this legacy has been dispersed with redevelopment among these streets. The sculptured figures flanking the High Street entrance to Wilson's Court are a case in point. Until a decade ago this facade existed as one of the more attractive covered approaches to the entries, but was removed in the course of rebuilding and replaced with an austere buttress of dull grey concrete. Incidentally, the Ann Street arch of Crown Entry underwent a similar alteration in recent times; it has been lowered some two feet by the addition of a sham arch which disguises the elegant proportions of the original brickwork – though the form of the old arch is still visible from inside the passageway.

Wilson's Court, High Street Facade, removed 1960s.

Crown Entry arch: exterior view from Ann Street.

Crown Entry arch: interior.

Many signboards, some of them most picturesque, have also been forfeited to renovations of one kind or another; but a worthy survivor – the Morning Star in Pottinger's Entry – remains in situ as a beacon to modern travellers with time on their hands, notwithstanding a rather inhibiting winged lion standing sentinel above the door. Heavy ironwork is scarce in the entries. Certainly very little of a decorative nature is to be seen, unless one regards the vermilion-painted corner railing and fluted skirting plate just inside the High Street entrance to Joy's Entry as such. High Street itself has an extremely solid iron fanlight still in position, allowing a measure of daylight to penetrate a dingy interior.

Victorian ironwork on Morning Star public house sign.

Corner railing, Joy's Entry.

Elsewhere are to be found remnants of abandoned gas lamp brackets, but one will look in vain for an intact fitment. The advent of the gas mantle brought elegance to a utilitarian need; it saw a combining of the purely functional with the aesthetic and encompassed in its life time the long Victorian age to which it inseparably belonged. Few items of nineteenth century street furniture had such affinity with their surroundings, and to the entries and byways of the town especially they brought an intimacy, not to say a homeliness, that remained after their usefulness came to an end.

Iron fanlight in High Street.

Ornamental arch, Crown Entry.

THE ENTRIES TODAY

For all their deep-rooted historical associations and their evident assimilation into the modern town, it is perhaps not unnatural to view the High Street entries as uneasy anachronisms of our age. Because much vital minutiae has already been lost to demolition and other changes (mostly of recent date), any proposal to preserve the entries as a kind of civic monument would scarcely be regarded as a feasible undertaking; though a selective approach to the issue could be both practical and timely.

Of the narrow streets in existence today, possibly Pottinger's Entry, with its mature enclosed approach from Ann Street and its remnants of eighteenth-century housing, might be considered worthy of attention from conservationists. The apparent anomaly of its surroundings - tall, dominant office blocks rising abruptly on either hand - serves to emphasise the antiquity of the old thoroughfare and isolate it as a microcosm amid a wider life pattern. Where official opinion is concerned, the Belfast City Planning Department is certainly aware of the intrinsic significance of the entries, though of necessity this takes the form of a broad-based, rather than specific, policy of controlled development. For example, a proposed new multi-storey car park to be sited between Pottinger's Entry and Church Lane will, if it becomes a reality, not be allowed to encroach on the entry itself, but can hardly fail to affect the overall character of the area. Even so, the intention to retain the entries as pedestrian precincts – there is definitely no plan to widen these narrow streets – is reassuring.

In practical terms, the function of the entries as public rights of way remains an important consideration; for such rights are in many instances of long standing duration. The inconvenience caused by the closure for security reasons in November 1972 of Sugarhouse Entry, the High Street entrances to Joy's Entry and Wilson's Court, and the restricted access through Crown Entry and Pottinger's Entry, has served to underline the utilitarian role of these passages. In 1959, correspondents in the local press complained that pedestrians were deprived of the old route across the bombed site of Sugarhouse Entry because of imminent redevelopment. Reaction of this kind is reminder enough of the indelible social attitudes that still hold sway regardless of time and circumstances.

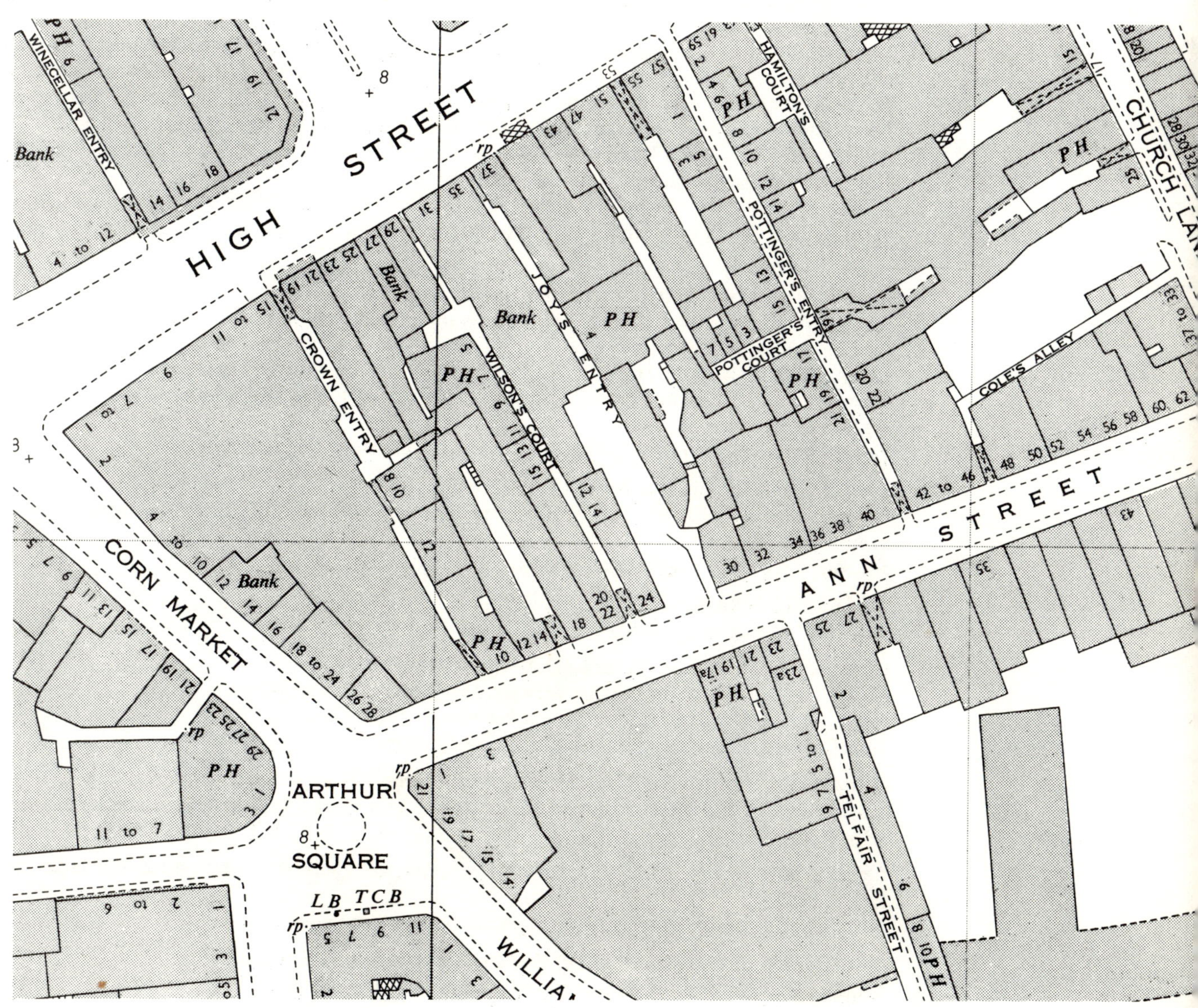

The High Street entries shown on the revised Ordnance Survey Map of 1965. (scale 1 inch to 110 feet) Crown copyright reserved.

APPENDIX

The word 'entry' is not unique to Belfast but is to be found in use in parts of Scotland and in several counties of England as well as in Ireland. For all that it is a locally familiar term its occurrence is not especially widespread, and it is merely one of many distinctive dialect words in regional use to describe structural features similar in appearance and function to the Belfast entries. Such features have long been an integral aspect of urban development and analogies of form and character are therefore to be expected wherever they occur. Cathal O'Byrne compared them to 'the little narrow ways that lie around the foot of Montmartre in Paris, the "vivas" of old Trastevere in Rome, the "vieux Carre" (the old French quarter of New Orleans in Louisiana), and the maze of connecting alleys that radiate from St Paul's churchyard in London'. Much earlier, James Makepeace Thackeray had also likened Belfast's High Street entries to those in parts of London.

The following list of selected dialect sources sets out many of the words encountered in various parts of Britain which may be regarded as synonymous with the Belfast entries.

English Dialect Dictionary, Joseph Wright (ed), 1905
Chare: Northumberland (*chair*), Durham, Warwickshire (*chewer*), Worcestershire, Gloucestershire (*chur*), Wiltshire (*chore*).
Entry: Northumberland, Durham, Yorkshire, Cheshire, Nottingham, Essex.
Ginnel: Scotland, Cumberland, Westmorland, Yorkshire, Lancashire, Cheshire.
Jetty: Leicestershire.
Tewer: Warwickshire (also *Tuer*), Gloucestershire, Oxfordshire (also *Ture*).

Leeds Dialect Glossary and Lore, J H Wilkinson, 1924
Entry: a covered passage in a row of houses; a passage between walls or even hedges, covered or not.
Snicket: a narrow passage, covered or not, between houses or walls.

Yorkshire Folk Tales, M C F Morris, 1892
Snig Cut: a short cut, originally a secret way.

Chambers' Scots Dialect Dictionary, A Warrack (ed), 1911
Entry: an alley or narrow passage between two houses; a house lobby.
Close: enclosed land; a farmyard; a narrow alley; a blind alley.
Wynd: a narrow lane or street; an alley; a small court.

A Glossary of Words used in Holderness, East Riding, F Ross, R Stead and T Holderness, 1877
Enthry: (north and west) a porch or entrance to a house; a short cul-de-sac, lane, or alley in a town.

Leicestershire Words, Phrases and Proverbs, collected by A B Evans; edited by Sebastian Evans, 1881
Jitty: a party passage or alley; a passage common to two houses.

New Glossary of the Dialect of the Huddersfield District, W E Haigh, 1928
Snikkit, Snekkit: a short cut, a narrow passage between houses or walls, saving a way round.

Entries, courts, etc, in the immediate vicinity of High Street, with their respective populations, according to the enumeration of Belfast's streets in 1823 contained in Benn's History of Belfast, published anonymously in that year.

Name	**Location**	**Population**
Bluebell Entry and Elbow Lane	Waring Street	150
Caddell's Entry	High Street	170
Cole's Alley and Mateer's Court	Church Lane	100
Cooney's Court	Ann Street	81
Crown Entry	High Street	70
Graham's Entry	High Street	137
Hamilton's Court	High Street	36
Joy's Entry and Joy's Court	High Street	112
Legg's Lane	High Street	29
Mitchell's Entry	High Street	61
Orr's Entry	High Street	48
Pottinger's Entry	High Street	191
Quin's Entry	High Street	11
Sugarhouse Entry (including Skipper Street)	High Street	142
Telfair's Entry	Ann Street	104
Wilson's Court	High Street	144
Winecellar Entry	High Street	30

Representative trades and professions of the High Street entries in 1840:

Matthew Kennedy, publican, Bluebell Entry
John Reid, lodgings, 6 Caddell's Entry
Robert Taylor, assistant crane master, 5 Cole's Alley
Owen McCann, fish monger, 22 Crown Entry
Thomas Lent, brushmaker, 7 Graham's Entry
James Smith, publican and sedan chair keeper, 12 Joy's Entry
Thomas McCann, bookbinder, 2 Joy's Court
Joseph McWilliams, innkeeper, 4 Legg's Lane
Alexander Nixon, shoemaker, 5 Mateer's Court
Arthur Saxton, tailor, 15 Mitchell's Entry
James Allen, tailoring establishment, 2 Orr's Entry
Marcus Ward, bookbinder and wholesale stationer, 14 Pottinger's Entry
Abraham Banbridge, tavern keeper, Sugarhouse Entry
James Burns, porter, 28 Telfair's Entry
Michael McCartney, house carpenter, 18 Wilson's Court
Hugh Armstrong, wine and spirit merchant, 5 Winecellar Entry

Population and commercial structure of Crown Entry in 1870 and 1972:

1870

1 J K Mitchel, hosier (back entrance)
3 Mrs Smith, dining rooms
5 W B Todd, oyster-house
7 W Linden, confectioner (back entrance)
9 M McMullen, chandler (back entrance)
11–13 T Kane, Crown Shellfish Tavern
15 T Clegg (back door)
12 Circus Hotel (back entrance)
10, 8 & 6 Morning News Office, R & D Read, printers and publishers
4 & 2 T Scott & Co, cabinet-makers (back entrance)

1972

1–13 F W Woolworth & Co (goods entrance)
4b Etam Ltd (goods entrance)
8 J Rice, commission agent
10–12 H McAlevey Ltd, commission agent
14 Capstan Lounge
16 McMahon Ltd (side door)

NOTES AND REFERENCES

1. Even at that time (1770), Pottinger's Entry was in all probability a very old thoroughfare; it had most certainly been in existence for a full half century – it appears on MacLanachan's map of 1715 as 'Pottinger's Lean' – and possibly a great deal longer. The family which gave its name to the entry was well established in the town by the latter half of the seventeenth century.
2. For further insight into actual living conditions encountered in these streets the reader is referred to *Walks among the Poor of Belfast* by W M O'Hanlon (1853; reprinted 1971). O'Hanlon deals with the mid-nineteenth century but his observations could well be related to the state of things a century earlier, allowing that population density was not then the critical factor it later became in the industrial sector.
3. Flooding was recorded in Ann Street in 1838: 'water up to Corn Market' – *Town Book of the Corporation of Belfast,* R M Young, 1892. Telfair's Entry: 'innundated to the depth of several feet' – *Belfast Fifty Years Ago,* T Gaffikin, 1875.
4. Information on name changes is fragmentary, though useful data is often to be gleaned from an examination of early maps, plans and surveys. Some such instances might be noticed here.

   The earliest 'entry' to be so named appears on MacLanachan's map of 1715: A 'Bullar's Entry' is shown leading off Broad Street (now Waring Street) more or less in line with the site of the present Donegall Street. The High Street passages are called 'leans' and 'alleys'; evidently the term 'entry' was a later suffix, though, as is clear from the solitary example on this map, it was certainly not unknown.

   A 'Plan of the Town of Belfast, 1757' shows Ann Street as Bridge Street; Corn Market as Shambles Street; Church Lane as Church Street. Another 'Plan' of the town in 1788 (by John Mulholland) places a 'Bulger's Entry' about the site of the present Joy's Entry, and among the several entries delineated on the north side of High Street are Mitchell's Entry, Addet's Entry, and two named Sugar House Lane. 'A Map of the Town and Environs of Belfast', surveyed in 1791 by James Williamson has the present Joy's Entry marked as McKitterick's Entry.

   Finally, a 'Survey of Belfast' in 1850, indicating the situation some eighty years earlier when the new Donegall leases were implemented, gives the name Pringle's Entry to the High Street end of Crown Entry. Cole's Alley is recorded as Little Lane; Joy's Entry as Change Alley (1767) and Exchange Alley (1826).
5. Of the extinct narrow streets perhaps none have given rise to greater general interest than Sugarhouse Entry, and a note on its origin may not be out of place here. The earliest reference to the site, before the entry itself came into being, goes back to 1678 when merchant George Macartney obtained a lease of 'Wilkinson's Tenement' extending over an area 126 ft by 42 ft on the piece of ground known as 'My Lady's Garden' from the Countess of Donegall. Macartney established a sugar refinery on the property and after a time the site was built up with an alignment of warehouses and offices. Possibly the entry took on definite form about the beginning of the eighteenth century, or even before, and if so can lay claim to being one of the earliest in the town and of similar antiquity to Pottinger's Entry. The original Sugarhouse was destroyed by fire in 1785, while the entry itself was reduced to rubble by the blitz of 5 May 1941. The site was cleared and later absorbed into the perimeter of the British Legion car park in High Street, but was reconstituted as a public right of way in 1960 after redevelopment. However, nothing of its former character survives.

   Sugarhouse Entry created an amount of literary interest in its eventful social and folk history. It was in a sense the classic entry, much quoted for its romantic connotations and recalled with affection by an older generation of Belfast people. Mention has been made of the picturesque pattern of life enacted within its walls, the human minutiae of which found its way into so many documented accounts of the old town.
6. Harriet Mellon, 1777–1837: Married Thomas Coutts, the banker, in 1815, and after his death inherited a large fortune. She became the Duchess of St Albans in 1827 upon her marriage to William Aubrey de Vere, the ninth duke. By all accounts she appears to have been a beautiful and socially acceptable woman, and numbered many influential personalities of the day among her friends. Three portrait paintings of Harriet Mellon – including one by Sir William Beechey – hang in the directors' room of Messrs Coutts Bank in London.
7. In 1972, only 300 gas lamps (maintained by three Corporation employees) remained in use in Belfast as the electrification of street lighting neared completion. Most of the entries were by that time lighted by electricity; Telfair Street still had three gas lamps of the five-mantle suspension type functioning, but due for replacement.

BIBLIOGRAPHY

Benn, G *History of Belfast,* 1877
Brett, C E B *Buildings of Belfast,* 1967
Cough, J *A Tour in Ireland,* 1814
Gaffikin, T *Belfast Fifty Years Ago,* 1875
Hayward, R *Belfast Through the Ages,* 1952
Hayward, R *In Praise of Ulster,* 1938
Jones, E *A Social Geography of Belfast,* 1960
MacCartian, H A *The Glamour of Belfast,* 1921
Millin, S S *Sidelights on Belfast History,* 1932
Millin, S S *Additional Sidelights on Belfast History,* 1938
Moore, A S *Old Belfast,* 1951
O'Byrne, C *As I Roved Out,* 1946
Owen, D J *History of Belfast,* 1921
Pilson, J A *History of the Rise and Progress of Belfast,* 1847
Pocock, R *A Tour in Ireland,* 1752
Strain, R W M *Belfast and its Charitable Society,* 1961
Thackeray, J M *An Irish Sketch Book,* 1842
Young, R M *The Town Book of the Corporation of Belfast,* 1892
Young, R M *Historical Notices of Old Belfast,* 1896

Newspaper articles, etc

Anon article 'Old Belfast By-ways', *Belfast News Letter,* 19 October 1927
Caughey, J 'Ann Street Actress became a Duchess', *Belfast News Letter,* 22 November 1962.
Loudan, J 'Alleys of Printing', *Belfast Telegraph,* 5 October 1962
Loudan, J 'Today Long Ago: Sugarhouse Entry', *Belfast Telegraph,* 5 May 1959.
Marshall, J J 'Amid the Haunts of Belfast's Old-time Conspirators', *Belfast Telegraph,* 9 January 1941.
Marshall, J J *Scrapbooks,* Linen Hall Library
O'Byrne, C 'A Famous Belfast Hostelry', *Irish News,* 22 April 1942
Robb, C J 'Sugarhouse Entry', *Irish News,* 20 January 1953
Robb, C J 'Sugarhouse Entry', *Irish News,* 26 February 1958
Robb, C J 'Sugarhouse Entry', *Belfast Telegraph,* 6 December 1955

ACKNOWLEDGMENTS

My thanks are due to the Ulster Museum for permission to reproduce a number of illustrations of old Belfast in this book; and to the Public Record Office of Northern Ireland for facilities to photograph the copy of MacLanachan's Map of 1715. I am also indebted to the Linen Hall Library for making valuable maps and plans of the town available for study and photography. Finally, mention must be made of source material on morphology supplied by Marguerita Oughton of Manchester; of the drawings of Telfair Street and Crown Entry contributed by Raymond Piper; and of the courtesy shown by various people during the preparation of this project.

EPILOGUE

A misplaced flora
fragmented plaster and eroded brick
change and decay
glassless, curtainless casements
restricted entry to the narrow streets

POTTINGE 'S
ENTRY
ACCESS
STRIANS
THIS POINT
CTION CORNMARKET./
CASTLE PL.
CLES
CTION CORNMARKET./
CASTLE PL.
HOURS
7AM-11PM
7AM-7AM
RESTRICTED

INDEX